Maxwell Nurnberg
with regards from
[illegible]

David McCord has also written:

FLOODGATE

THE CROWS

A STAR BY DAY

FAR AND FEW *(verse for children)*

THE OLD BATEAU AND OTHER POEMS

ODDLY ENOUGH

STIRABOUT

H.T.P. — PORTRAIT OF A CRITIC

AN ACRE FOR EDUCATION

ABOUT BOSTON

BAY WINDOW BALLADS

AND WHAT'S MORE

TWELVE VERSES FROM XII NIGHT

ON OCCASION

He has edited:

ONCE AND FOR ALL

WHAT CHEER

ODDS WITHOUT ENDS

ODDS WITHOUT ENDS

by David McCord

Little, Brown and Company
Boston · Toronto

LIBRARY OF CONGRESS CATALOG CARD NO. 54-5139

FIRST EDITION

Certain of the poems in this book have appeared in various magazines and in one newspaper: twenty-one in the *Atlantic,* eighteen in *The New Yorker,* six in *Harper's,* three in the *Saturday Review,* and others in the *Harvard Alumni Bulletin, The Harvard Lampoon, The General Magazine and Historical Chronicle* of the University of Pennsylvania, *The Month at Goodspeed's, The University of Kansas City Review, Your Field Sports* published by Wildlife Conservation, Inc., of Boston, *Wine and Food* of London, and *The Boston Globe.* I have to thank the various editors and proprietors of these publications for permission to reprint.

The poems on the following pages were first printed in *The New Yorker:* 4, 5, 6, 8, 10, 11, 24, 27, 39, 41, 42, 55, 65, 86, 99, 131, 132, 134; Copyright 1941, 1943, 1945, 1947, 1949, 1950, 1951, 1952, 1953, by The New Yorker Magazine, Inc.

Published simultaneously in Canada
by Little, Brown & Company (Canada) Limited

PRINTED IN THE UNITED STATES OF AMERICA

To
Philip Sanford Marden

Nugis addere pondus

Acknowledgments

I should like in particular to express my thanks to Glenn C. Bramble for giving me the notion that something might be made of *Nottoway* and *thataway;* to Norman L. Dodge for a bookman's hospitality to a casual customer; to Professor Sculley Bradley and William James for productive encouragement and for their interest in certain poems; and to Walter M. Whitehill for his generous part in publishing as a birthday broadside under the imprint of the Club of Odd Volumes the gastronomic nonsense called "Remembrance of Things Passed." As one born at 9 East 10th Street in New York City, I hasten to identify W.R.B. and C.M. in "A Brace of Squabs" as William Rose Benét and Christopher Morley. *Alijug* in "Keep Your Distance" is pronounced Ali*juke,* as in the box. For those concerned with Musgrave Rituals, may I say that "animula vagula glandula" was committed to the fragment in which it now stands perhaps ten years before I saw it (I think) in one of Conrad Aiken's poems: a minor case of converging evolution. The stout quotation from Horace for my old friend the prior of Saint Botolph is from *Epistles:* I, 19, line 42 — "To give weight to trifles."

Verse has many forms:
A hundred different norms.
Norms are an awful curse
And paralyze one's verse.

Contents

Ept and Ert

Hanging Indentures

Three Colicky Bucolics

Cantabrigian

Wings and Things

Ept and Ert

Gloss

I know a little man both ept and ert.
An intro-? extro-? No, he's just a vert.
Sheveled and couth and kempt, pecunious, ane,
His image trudes upon the ceptive brain.

When life turns sipid and the mind is traught,
The spirit soars as I would sist it ought.
Chalantly then, like any gainly goof,
My digent self is sertive, choate, loof.

Nightmare in a Museum

Then the glance slants
To the jade blade
With the gilt hilt
In the shade made
By the chance stance
Of the Ming King
In the tomb gloom
Of the Sing Wing.

And the lawn yawns
In the dark park
Where the tawn fawns
Are the stark mark
On the ground round,
And the bronze swans
Like a boat float.

From the soy boy
Comes the drowned sound
Of a throat note:
Myrna Loy Loy!

Grand Tour

His glasses broke at Brokenbow,
He changed a tire at Lost Mule Flat,
He drank a Coke in Kokomo
And Bisodol in Medicine Hat.

There was no sleep at Sabbath Rest,
In Waterproof it rained quite hard;
Lo Lo is higher than he guessed.
You ever et at Cheesequake, pard?

He did some work in Shirkieville,
Sweated in Frozen, froze in Fry;
Called it a day in Half Day, Ill.,
And fled from Brave, bade Sweet good-by.

Tuesday in Monday, stranger to Strange,
Christmas for Easter, perhaps Maybee;
Zap on the map was a welcome change
From chowder in Clam and coffee in Tea.

Lonely in Only, sickly in Slick,
Better in Best, but down in Drain;
Soso in Oso, dead in Quick,
In Stamping Ground he's home again.

Fugitive from Chess

People always say to me, "Do you play chess?"
I don't know why they do it, for the answer isn't "Yes."
I know what chess boys look like: they have long white beards and gout.
But still, that doesn't tell me why they corner me and shout:

"Do you play chess?"
(Expecting I'll say, "Yes.")
No, sir, I don't. I can't.
I haven't, and I shan't.
I think I know a pawn —
Or maybe it's a prawn;
I know a knight
(Red, black, or white);
I know a castle, I know a queen;
But lots of others in between
I don't know, though I might.
No, sir, I don't play chess —
Can't you look at me and guess?
But thank you for the compliment. Good night.

"Thank you for the compliment" — that's something else amiss.
Why must I make apologies and carry on like this?
I might have learned to play The Game. I might speak Russian, too.
I might have split the atom, but I left those things for you.

Do *I* play chess?
What misery to confess!
My buoyant spirit dies,
I speak with lowered eyes

And shiver in the shame
Of "Sorry, not my game."
It isn't that I mind
This side of me that's blind;
It's being thought
I'm one who ought
To play that galls me so.
Why can't I say,
"Old man, go 'way!
Play chess? Of course not. *No!*"

Traveling once to Halifax, I rose before the dawn.
I washed and shaved and thought about my breakfast later on.
One other man had risen too, and as the murky day
Disclosed the lonely Maritimes, that's what I heard him say:

"Do *you* play chess?"
And then the old distress . . .
I've seen a man turn round,
Cross over with a bound —
Excitement in his eye
And in his mind a "Why,
By God, I nearly missed
This obvious strategist
Who, like as not, can play
Twelve men at once all day."
And why should it be so?
It is. You want to bet?
(Here comes one now. All set?)
"Do you play chess? Yes?"
"*No!*"

Up with the Lark, Down with the Doldrums!

Agreeable to me the nascent day:
Ham, eggs, black coffee, buttered toast, and jam.
And to the pig his corn, the horse his hay;
To ewes, the cry of ewe-hoo! from the lamb.

Acceptable to me the languorous dark:
The switches off, the covers up, come sleep.
And to the cat her fence, the dog his bark;
To ewes their usefulness as counted sheep.

Give a Rouse—Give a Rauhaus!

I bowed to the brains of the Bauhaus.
"Hauhaus it going?" I said.
He winced at the glance of his spauhaus.
"It goes." And the joke was dead.

The sun shines hotter in Tauhaus;
The god on the sundeck says "*What?*"
"Too hot for man or mauhaus,"
I murmur. The joke is not got.

I grin as another would grauhaus:
But done with the Bauhaus am I.
So any old sauhaus or lauhaus
Can try it. "Hauhaus it . . . ?" *You* try.

Highboy, Lowboy, Oboy!

"Come, my love, and let us stoppë
In our ancient jade jaloppë
At ye oldë moldë shoppë:
Fine Antiques — to Sell or Swappë.
Out you hoppë, in we poppë."

"Lawsy, what a table toppë!"
"Lazy Susan? That's a coppë."
"Grant's old razor!" "Where's the stroppë?"
"Snuffbox . . . Pewter . . . London foppë."
"Flip glass." "Careful, now. Don't droppë!"

See that curious, *curious* moppë!"
"Buggy whips — the old clip-cloppë
Days!" "A pruning knife, to loppë?"
"Burbank owned it." "Will you ploppë
Down five bucks for these sweet sloppë
Jars?" "That's much too much — *de troppë!*"

O! As in Oblivion

The pterodactyl ceased to fly
And man has ever wondered why;
Tyrannosaurus cooked his goose
For reasons that appear abstruse;

Deep in an Eocenic sea
The Zeuglodon's an absentee;
The trilobite by trillions quit,
Perhaps because he didn't fit,

And something slew the giant sloth
Ere Job beheld the behemoth.
But does it matter? Yes, it does:
You can't revive the *is* in *was*.

The roc and griffin never *were* —
The lucky him, the lucky her!
And that, at least in part, explains
Their lack of petrified remains.

All footed, finned, and feathered things
Had better beat feet, fins, and wings;
And they that wriggle, inch, or crawl
Had better hump their underall.

The fossil years without a doubt
Bear witness that we're going out
Lock, stock, and barrel, hip and thigh:
And this means you, and this means I.

Treasure Trove

I dug beneath an apple tree
And spaded up a piece of spode,
Two pine-tree shillings, and the free
Translation of a runic ode.

I dug again, and in the clod
Appeared an artifact, a shell,
An inlaid toothpick, and some odd
Rude smelling salts without the smell.

They say that when the moon is white
As blossoms on that apple tree,
A man is digging all the night.
The legend doesn't mention me.

A Clutch of Clerihews

1

The Keystone cops
Were simply tops,
And a bit more spry
Than the private eye.

2

A "hey nonny nonny"
Means everything's bonny.
But "tara diddle dyno?"
Damned ifyno.

3

Modern Art
Has made a good start.
But so has a comet
And the urge to vomit.

4

The bathysphere,
As I see it from here,
Means a pressurized role
For the goldfish bowl.

5

The heath hen
Will not be seen again.
She kicked the bucket
On Nantucket.

6

Spinoza,
I observe *sub rosa,*
Has only to philosophize
And the brain ossifies.

7

Poor Richard to Ben:
"Will you lend me your pen?"
"You go fly a kite!
And how would I write?"

8

Gertrude Stein
Hewed to the line;
But about the hewer
I'm not so shewer.

On the Double

The postman ringing twice my bell
Announces all for him is well;
And then must I rush down to see
If all is likewise well for me.

To a Certain Most Certainly Certain Critic

He takes the long review of things;
He asks and gives no quarter.
And you can sail with him on wings
Or read the book. It's shorter.

Any Day Now

Johnny reading in his comic
Learned to handle the atomic.
Johnny blew us all to vapors.
What a lad for cutting capers!

Hot Rod

Hitch not your beachless wagon to a star.
Unlikely, son, that you will fare so far.
A star is such a dusty little grain,
And loftiness to you is high octane.

Hand Me That Chisel

He wrote like Spenser, archaic to his time:
He thought like Darwin, shocking for his day:
He walked like Dante, touched with the sublime:
At night he got undressed and hit the hay.

Early American

1

The Nottoway
Never got away
To the Platte away
Out thataway.

2

The Shoshone
Often rode a pony.
It has never been shoshown
That he rode a pone.

3

For quite a spell
The Algonquin had no hotel,
An idea to which the tribe
Didn't subscribe.

4

The Cliffdweller
Was an odd feller;
And also, I hasten
To add, a mason.

5

The Ute
Lived over the butte
From the Hopi
Who thought he was dopi.

6

Sitting Bull
Rarely got full.
He just sat
And got fat.

Daedalus, Stay Away from My Transom!

The age of flight, the age of flight:
They say it hasn't come yet quite.
The atom somehow got between,
And something else may intervene
Before a man can wear his wings
The way he wears his socks and things,
Or jet-propel himself from here
To points beyond the stratosphere.
But still, the experts all agree,
The age of flight is what we'll see;
It's what we'll get, it's what we'll be.
  All right, all right:
  If flight means flee —
  That's me.

What is there in this age of flight
To make me hug the earth so tight?
The age of flint, the age of stone
Developed from the age of bone,
And in the prehistoric dawn
Our fathers met them axehead on.
The age of iron, brass, and tin
And other ages trickled in.
The age of coal, the age of steam
Were mutual, like milk and cream.
The age of coal and steam, alas,
Expanded to an age of gas;
And then, as if that wouldn't do,
The age of Edison came through.
So now, with this atomic age,

You think we've turned the final page?
Not yet, my friend: the ceiling height
Is coming with the age of flight.
I think about it day and night
    All right, all right,
    For flight means flee
    To me.

I do not want a pair of wings
And supersonic underthings.
I do not care to cross the street
Retracting, as I fly, my feet.
I do not want O'Malley's gift;
I don't desire that kind of lift.
I do not long for rocket ships
And outer interstellar trips.
I'm glad they have canals on Mars:
I'm sorry that the moon has scars.
It's comforting to think that space
May hide the meistermaster race
On some far planet, and contrast
My foolish future with their past.
The age of flight is food for thought:
I haven't eaten as I ought.
Out on a limb, this earthbound tree
Just suits me to a Model T —
It's plenty high enough for me
    All right, all right.
    And flightless me
    I'll be.

May I Give You a Lift?

Elevators are queer devices:
They carry you up and down in trices.
If marked *Express,* as their speed increases,
They carry you up and down in pieces.

Elevators are commonplaces,
Lacking the lure of the open spaces,
Full of corrective impetuses.
The view is better from Greyhound Busses.

Elevators are not for cruises —
You take the one that the starter chooses.
Elevators are full of pauses
Analogous to suspended clauses.

Elevators produce neurosis,
Claustrophobia, metempsychosis.
Elevators are hits and misses
Along the faces of precipices.

O Bonny Dundee, Who Is Honoring Thee?

Honey of heather, tartan of the clans,
Rind of a lazy long. and milder lat.:
Eggs boil, toast tans,
The percolator perkles *pffut-pffut-pffat,*
And there you are
In the old familiar white black-lettered jar.

Keiller & Sons: No want of toasted buns;
Of hot bread, English muffins, biscuits, rolls:
Count us the lucky ones!
Men may have lost their hemispheric souls,
But under oak and deodar,
By birch and palm and gloomy grot,
Why there you are
In the old English white black-lettered pot.

Dundee! you need and want no praise from me:
What could I give or add to you?
"Grand Medal of Merit Vienna '73,"
"Only Prize Medal for Marmalade London '62."
Quite prominent they are
On the clear white black-lettered jar.

Nothing since then? when sour, sordid men
Sweeten their bleak unlettered lives with what,
Old dears, *mijnheers,*
They've found God knows how many years
Goes to the spot —
The amber-ember symbol of the Scot?

Time for another major Medal, boys!
You've made — forgive the phrase — the grade
  (Gold *this* time: no alloys) .
"Only Prize Medal for Marmalade UN"
                                        Forever!
  For never in the trade
A sweeter drop on top of toast. But most
  This Sunday-Dundee morning, here you are
In the old white and bold-black-lettered jar.

Sore Finger Exercise

Aladdin, odd but comfortable in "d"s,
And *benefiting,* chary of two "t"s,
Or *desiccate,* a dry bed full of "c"s:
Mnemosyne, what have you such as these?

Inoculate and *innuendo,* true,
Defend, in turn, too many from too few;
Sappho appeases, and the "w"
In *powwow* winds a writhen tirraloo.

And "h," when *unwithheld,* was all surprise
Till *skiing* won the slalom of the eyes.
Trekking and *chukker* smack of other skies;
Old *syzygy* has *obbligato* "y"s.

"Men Never Weary of Women with Brains"*

Men are queer creatures, as history explains:
They work in the day and raise hell in the dark;
They live in the cities, in mountains, on plains —
And better that Noah had sunk with his ark,
For a terrible flame's the result of a spark;
We've a shortage of Abels, a crowding of Cains.
But still it is cheering to hear the remark
That men never weary of women with brains.

Men are queer creatures — the fact still remains.
Their skin is too thin or it's tough as a bark;
With sulphur and treacle and such in their veins,
They are kind as a cow or as mean as a shark.
They sleep until noon or get up with the lark;
They give and they take of those infinite pains.
You could hand them an A or an E for a mark,
Adding: men never weary of women with brains.

Men are queer creatures: for one who abstains,
A thousand fly off on the funniest arc;
The paradox is they are all bound by chains
To the petty, the mean, to the empty, the stark.
On paper they're hunting some blonde little Snark,
Or figuring losses, forgetting the gains.
Would you guess, when you see them at work in the park,
That men never weary of women with brains?

* Dorothy Dix in *The Boston Globe*.

Envoy

Prince, it is footless to fuss, fret, or cark.
Put it: man, like his scutcheon, is smeary with stains.
And that's why it's cleansing to hear . . . hear it? *Hark!*
Yes, men never weary of women with brains.

Eroica

Straight to the point he came. The point withdrawn,
He hit the nail square on its phantom head.
He spoke his mind when listeners had gone:
The issues that he faced were always dead.

He stood his ground if nothing was opposed,
Raised a sharp question that could not be heard,
And saw the opening when the door was closed.
The fire is out. His ashes may be stirred.

New Twilight on Old Gods

(Symmetrics)

I

Sisyphus, rolling up the hill his stone,
Found that he could not make the grade
alone: alone
Today the best of us say this of us,
We are no better rollers than was Sisyphus.

II

Atlas at last unable to sustain
The heavens' weight sank down to earth
again: again
We cry for someone huge and hatless.
You'll have to bear the world though, this time, Atlas!

III

Pandora never has received our praise
For singling out the lid that she did
raise: raise
Every lid, the eyelid first. Sand or a
Speck of dust can hide like Hope, Pandora.

IV

Calypso *ipso facto* played it cool;
Penelope employed the golden
rule: rule
Out old Zeus, for whom the gods eclipse so
Easily is always a Calypso.

V

Poseidon, Greek for Neptune, has in hand
The trident as he rides from sea to
land: land
Sakes, old fellow, look which way you're ridin'!
Much better off at sea these days, Poseidon.

VI

Calliope, concerned with eloquence,
How graciously you lived one present
tense: tents
Of another kind your recent tie-up, he
Is younger now who loves you so, Calliope.

Keep Your Distance

Old Mr. Meggs the ultimate
In dégagé climbs out of bed:
In time and space he twirls a bit
And visions filter through his head.

Three thousand miles to El Ferrol
(The man looks up as though addressed)
And millions to the sun. Old Sol,
He says, and buttons up his vest.

Six thousand-odd from Alijug
The sextant wavers on a star.
He nods and swallows the rebuke
And ambles for the nearest bar.

His brother out in Illinois
Has written — but nine hundred miles!
The steak is ready to enjoy:
Old Mr. Meggs embarks with smiles.

A pleasant ride to Olean,
Though distance varies in New York.
Take this from plate to mouth: the man
Annihilates it with his fork.

Remember, sir, the Isle of Hope?
Cartographers have never fixed
Its true position. Meggs's *Nope*
Sounds half between and half betwixt.

Slightly Foxed; or, a Letter to a Bookseller

I wrote you for a copy of *The Ox*.
I quote: "Two vols., de luxe, calf, mint in box."
It seems to look like other minted books:
What kind of looking makes a book de luxe?
I might have bought that other one, *The Quilt:*
"Small 4to, buckram, vellum backstrip, gilt";
Or something else unscattered from a set.
(Who was that man who wrote *The Sea is Wet?*)
Comes now *The Ox* for which you send a bill.
Find me the second volume, if you will —
A yoke of oxen. Let it be full calf.
Whoever saw an ox installed in half?

All Sette? Go Slo!

My fond *ue* is clipped from catalog,
And program lets me down or leaves me flat.
Supposing I turned polywog to frogue,
Or came out clean for clamme? Would they like that?

Shoppës have cashiered cheque; coupé is coup;
Only the king's assize saved cigarette.
For all I care, toupee can be a toup!
Good nite, swete Prince, I'm thru, tho glad we mette.

Sanctuary

Lo, the poor Indian, and
Gladly, the cross-eyed bear:
How many years have I known them,
This never enfranchised pair!
They, the two disembodied
Survivors of common ground,
Live or have lived in *lapsus*
Linguae — suspicious sound.
Now from the orthographic
Realm of their kith and kin
Cry, the beloved country,
Is here to take them in.

Hanging Indentures

To the Lido with Fido

DOG IS NO BAR TO EUROPE TRAVEL; LARGER LINERS PROVIDE KENNELS

Your dog may even pick up a bit of French, if you travel on the French Line. For there is a special menu for dogs. A sample from the liner *Liberté* follows:

Le Plat de Tayaut
(Consommé de boeuf — toasts — légumes)

La Préférence du Danois
(Os de côte de boeuf, de jambon et de veau)

Le Régime Végétarien des Dogs
(Tous les légumes frais et toutes les pâtes alimentaires)

Le Régal de Sweekey
(Carottes — viande hachée — épinards — toasts)

— New York *Herald Tribune*
World Travel Guide

Le Plat de Tayaut

Bon voyage, Tayaut, my best of breed!
Improve your French, and ere you feed
On clear, well-croutonned consommé,
Regard the napkin on the tray,
Propose the toast, and drink to me
Who thought you might enjoy the sea.

La Préférence du Danois

Great Dane, or Danny Boy, you'll find
The bones you buried far behind
In New Rochelle will not compare
With French Line canine bill-of-fare.
For oh, *les os* of beef and ham
And veal! Or don't you give a damn?

Le Régime Végétarien des Dogs

Whose vegetarian Scotty pup
Will this *Régime* inspire to sup?
Is not such farinaceous salve
Too heavy, like the accent *grave?*
It seems the proper slop for hogs.
(Be careful how you *pâte des Dogs!*)

Le Régal de Sweekey

Here, Sweekey! As you sail afar,
Regale yourself with *épinards,*
The best champagne, *viande hachée* —
For every dog must have his day.
Not every dog, though, has the chance
To disembark in French in France.

Perchance to Dream

(I'm taking no perchances)

"Professor H. B. McGlade, of Ohio State University, found that there were a number of foods that were almost sure-shot dream producers in a large percentage of persons . . . : fresh pineapple, bananas, cucumbers and watermelon. (Mix them all together and we guarantee a nightmare!) " — From "What You Eat Tells What You Are" by John E. Gibson.

— *This Week Magazine,* August 31, 1952

"Waiter," I said, "another slice of melon."
How could *I* know the fellow was a felon?
And yet I deem it odd that I should dream
And wake up screaming as he said, "Don't scream!"
(Perhaps you deem it odd that I should deem.)

Pineapple is pleasant, and I ate it
Fresh with some sugar. Now, of course, I hate it.
I dreamt that I was happy in Hawaii,
When up he came. "Aloe," he said. "Good-bii."
(Straightening his tie and dotting the double ii.)

Bananas? Not for me, thanks to that waiter!
He brought them fried, and some six hours later
We robbed a blind man and a small saloon.
A bank was next, but I woke up too soon.
(Ability to wake is quite a boon.)

A little tarragon on sliced cucumber
And I was off to deep, disastrous slumber.
I dreamt of *Moby Dick:* filet of fluke.
"Waiter!" I cried. He smiled a mild rebuke.
"Waiter!" That's all . . . His blackjack was a cuke.

More E. Power Biggs to You!

(9:30 A.M. every Sunday: E. Power Biggs, organist; Station WEEI & a National Network)

Twice as merry as grigs
When E. Power Biggs
Plays Handel round nine of an A.M.,
We limber the brush
In the lathery hush
Of release from life's murder and mayhem.

Out of bed, feeling tops,
As he pulls at the stops
Or strolls up and down on the basses,
We button our sleeves
In the absence of Jeeves
And forget the mad world he erases.

Pass the sugar and cream
As the powerful stream
Flows over the beam to the tonic!
Let the coffee be hot
When he reaches that spot —
And our soul the divine supersonic.

Counterpoint, counterpain,
In the van, in the vein,
He is strong, he is true, he is tender.
He has flutes, he has drums,
He has fingers and thumbs;
He has feet — and they're ready to render.

Nothing mean, nothing small,
Nothing bilious at all,
When Biggs begs the best of a theme. O
Humana! Thy Vox
Cries a plague and a pox
On the sleepers asleep and a-dream-o!

Unsteady as You Go

The general motion of the planets through the sky from day to day is west to east, the same as for the sun and moon.

— New York *Herald Tribune*

Young Lochinvar came out of the West,
But outer China 'crost the Bay
Something comes up like thunder, guessed
By Kipling to be dawn or day.
I somehow feel oppressed to find
The damned thing coming up behind:
I had it settled in my mind.
(I must be blind.)

And by the way,
Before I leaves:
What says the *Trib*
Of Adam's rib —
Eve's?

The Absent Treatment of Walter Pater

Shelley's a trade-mark used on sheets . . .
— Sir John Squire

The poet Morris is a chair,
  Lord Kelvin's now a Kelvinator;
Lister is a mouthwash. Where
  Is honor done to Walter Pater?

Burns' ashes stick to his cigar,
  The name of Pasteur's writ in milk;
Chief Pontiac's a damn good car.
  Why isn't Pater of their ilk?

Beatty and Nelson — both hotels;
  Grant's a tomb; Lee, half a college;
Bell's a system. Nothing sells
  Us Walter Pater to my knowledge.

Audubon? He's a feeding ground;
  Lindbergh a light; a canyon, Bryce;
La Guardia's a field; but round
  The world, poor Pater! Still no dice.

Lincoln? a highway; George? a lake;
  McKinley? mountain; Jackson? park;
Franklin? an institute. Why stake
  Old Walter out there in the dark?

Fame beckons. One becomes a dam,
  A bridge, a watch, a kind of cheese,
A process, or a safety pram.
  My client — he is none of these.

Industry! Public Works! Whose fault?
  The sacred cows are *all* in clover.
Is Pater worth his attic salt?
  It's just an idea . . . think it over.

By Swancoote Pool

Going back more years than I care to remember brings me to a sultry July afternoon when Arthur called and suggested we try the tench at Swancoote Pool, and to it (with desire for its peace rather than the fishing) we slowly cycled. Of the many baits with which tench can be caught we found lightly ledgering with wasp grub usually gave the best results and so in accordance with usual practice we soon got going opposite our favourite lily beds.

— *Confessions of a Carp Fisher* by "BB."
Eyre and Spottiswoode, London, 1950

The genial wasp provides the grub,
The tench provide the fun;
Eschewing roach, carp, dace, and chub,
I crouch behind a leafy shrub
And ledge them one by one:
  Grandfather, father, son.
  So easy is it done.

And lightly ledgering anon —
Whatever that may be —
Into a quiet world withdrawn,
My hypertension goes — is gone
With every tasty tench I see
  Until it's time for tea.
  Then lily bed for me.

Cash Me, Encash Me Again!

In July many of us, like the sunflower, turn towards the sun. As holidays approach, arrangements have to be made, and here the Midland Bank can help, not least by providing for the encashment of your cheques at a branch near to where you will be staying, and by looking after your valuables and documents while you are away. — Advertisement of the Midland Bank Limited.

— *The Times Literary Supplement*, London, July 6, 1951

I wrote a check, and in the bank
I sought encashment of the same.
The young enteller's look was blank;
He took the cheque and read my name.

The manager was called, bespoke
A word or two. When I produced
Credentials of a sort, a joke
Was made. No laughter was enloosed.

"Your cheque?"
"My check."
Of no account,
Apparently, the stranger had
Enchanced to write the large amount
Of fifty bucks. The news was bad.

Correct! No fifty bucks, no dice.
I shuffled off and made my stand
At Mike's Enporium. Very nice.
I left with my encash enhand.

"In Candent Ire"; or, Call Off Your Dogma, Catherine!

"Above all it is well to know his father, the sturdy Yankee who wrote bad verse and good books . . ." — From the opening page of the foreword to *Yankee from Olympus* by Catherine Drinker Bowen.

He wrote good books, he wrote bad verse;
The One-Hoss Shay became his hearse,
And rattling toward oblivion:
"Farewell," we cried, and he was gone.
Then here's to Catherine Bowen —
Drinker Bowen, Drinker Bowen!
For curious the seeds that she be sowin',
She be sowin'.
And singular the things that she be knowin',
She be knowin'!

He wrote bad verse, he wrote good books;
Which sounds to me as though it brooks
No argument. Well, tit for tat,
The good ones were *The Autocrat.*
Still, here's to Catherine Bowen —
Drinker Bowen, Drinker Bowen!
In many ways it's praise we be bestowin',
Be bestowin'!
But there's one little debt that she be owin',
She be owin'!

He wrote good books, he wrote bad verse.
Well, some of us could do much worse
Than take the best of all the bad
And, had we written it, be glad.

While here's to Catherine Bowen —
Drinker Bowen, Drinker Bowen!
Who knows where *Mr. Justice* Holmes is goin',
Holmes is goin',
Every minute — since for him the horn's worth blowin',
Horn's worth blowin'!

He wrote good verse, he made bad puns.
Say *that,* and she will put the son's
Old father in a better light;
Herself a little nearer right.
So here's to Catherine Bowen —
Drinker Bowen, Drinker Bowen!
In wine the doctor liked to see a-flowin',
See a-flowin'!
And may the doctor make a better showin',
Better showin'
(With the author's permission
In the next edition).

Let's Not Call a Spud a Spud

Fishing at the Norfolk Trout Ponds opened officially on March 18, 1950. The cold weather and ice did not deter a goodly number of fishermen eager to be at the rainbows and brookies.

— *Your Field Sports,* March–April 1950

Since squaretails now are brookies,
'Tis on the cards and bookies
Chinooks shall be Chinookies.
So pass the cakes and cookies!
With pwitty flies on hookies
I'm off for haunts and nookies
Where lurk the Aroostookies.

Fido Bites Fog

Fido (fog intensive dispersal of) took a large bite of fog out of the skies of Southern California last night and won acclaim as a marked step forward in the progress of commercial aviation throughout the world.

— Boston Daily Globe

Lie down, Fido.
Lie down, dog!
Down, sir,
Lie down!
Good dog,
That's a good dog.

Fido speaking:
Sit up, fog!
Up, sir,
Sit up!
Good fog;
That's a good fog.

Prince of Truffles

A fifty-year record for these parts [Massalombarda, Italy] was broken today when Grisetta, Francisco Monti's little dog, pawed up a truffle that weighed almost three and one half pounds.

It won for Monti the local title of "Prince of Truffles," held for years by Giovanni Tozzolo. His dog dug up a three-pound truffle years ago.

A truffle is an edible underground fungus considered by some to be a great delicacy.

— New York *Herald Tribune*

Tozzolo said his truffle weighed three pounds.
Dog dug it up. Three pounds or a truffle more.
Now comes Grisetta, princess of the hounds,
Who paws away for Monti *pour le sport.*

O beauful truffle, claiming three-point-five
(Massalombarda's) in de col' col' groun'!
O rueful Gio Tozzolo, if alive,
Meet Monti, whose pup upped him to the crown.

Reassurance

After glancing through more than one hundred newspaper clippings from a service bureau, each consisting of this single line: "Harvard College Library dates back to 1638."

I do not say the old days will return;
I know the Age of Flight means my eclipse;
That's why I feel such beautiful concern
For what is pasted on these pale pink slips.

"O world, O life, O time!" — as Shelley said:
Let *Life* and *Time* descry the world's sad fate;
But as for me, I think I'll think instead
On what dates back to 1638.

Fair Harvard! — no whit fairer than the line,
"Harvard College Library, et cetera . . ."
Eh? Something clean, traditional, and fine
About it — homogeneous, not hetera.

And better still, its truth has been proclaimed
Across the land. O seminal sweet spark!
You've lit the minds of Hibbing, Minn., reclaimed
The soul of Alton, Ill., Fayetteville, Ark.

Beatrice, Neb., is yours (as one could wish);
Salina, Kas., and Popular Bluff, Mo.
Yours Lubbock, Tex., and Escanaba, Mich.,
Nogales, Ariz., Lawton, Okla. No?

Yes, yes! Such evidence is not in vain:
For I observe behind this epic fact
Our roots of iron, and that we are sane —
And I alive, emeritus, intact.

Where Is My Butterfly Net?

When baby wakes the woolly spread
That held him warmly in his bed,
Shows little humps, where tiny feet
Make patterns underneath the sheet!
And, oh, his hands seek friendly things —
Like butterflies with frail, sweet wings . . .

— Margaret E. Sangster in a
Libby's Baby Foods advertisement

When baby woke in woolly spread,
"Give me some butterflies," he said.
"And since I'm clumsy with these things,
Give me an extra set of wings."

A Brace of Squabs

Poetry Package, by W.R.B. and C.M. Introduction by Cuckoo. The poems are signed P.C. (Pigeon Cove) and D.D. (Dove Dulcet).

Comes now from the small end of plenty's horn
A package gift-wrapped on the New Year's morn —
A fragment of the street where I was born.

The address clearly 51 E. 10:
The packaging performed by some small wren,
The packaged poems the dovecote work of men —

P.C., D.D.: Prize pair of homing birds!
The phoenix-nesting hatcher of fine words
And Don Dove Dulcet singing here in thirds.

Much have I trammeled in the realms of gold!
Pease porridge hot is not pease porridge cold:
So careful I to buy and not be sold.

Were I to lay my Truman dollar down
To hear the singing of my native town,
This is my title, adjective and noun:

"Poetry Package!" What an odd conceit
To issue from so personal a street:
So small, so imbric, and so passing neat.

The Cuckoo, advocating these two bards,
Aware in what affection they are pards,
Pipes of the Urn which they have filled with shards.

And, if my little metaphors will mix,
I'll match them shard to shard, no cicatrix
To show the joining when the rubric thicks:

Two poets in one poem. I quote in part
In full: "A door stands open in the heart
And all good things are true." Then what is art

Without this door to open as we please
And let the poet out to flout and tease;
Let him indwell, a rug across his knees?

Dove Dulcet and his Pigeon Cove are twain
For whom intensity is more than pain,
For whom no chill could presuppose the blain;

In whom true elevation of the soul
Is no small sunflash in the goldfish bowl,
With whom the solemn still becomes the droll.

"I saw my youth, a moment, from the sky . . ."
And in a bus the other riding by
Distills Metropolis in raindrops.
Aye,

From Forty-second Street (above, below)
The "bursting birds sing seltzer." Morwenstowe
And Natty Bumppo — each is apropos.

I doff my hat: "*And still the cock doth crow!*"

Three Colicky Bucolics

Back Tomorrow

Come now what may,
The mind is fluttery.
The brook has much to say:
Gay, guttery.
Flowers are fresh and fey,
Birds uttery;
And I seem, in my way,
More muttery.

Up, down, over hills,
This leftside battery
Discharges, charges, fills
My creaking clattery
Carcass with new gills
Of pure plasmattery
Chemic for old ills,
For teeth too chattery.

Far in the van,
Bright wings are flittery,
Tail feathers brake and fan;
From the nest the twittery
Sound that we say began
In the saurian-crittery
World before man
Denies the jittery.

Death to the shrike!
So I, a votary
Not of the mike
Nor of man the motory,

Do what I like.
To clinic and coterie,
Off on a hike
Is my antidotary.

Armored Division

I stopped my walk
Just to watch a hawk.
Then I turned from speed
To an airborne seed,
And I saw for man
How it all began.

For a chute of silk
Is the milkweed's milk
And the maple's crop
Is a feathered prop.
In the pitcher plant's lap
There's a booby trap.

The sensitive plant
(May it long enchant)
Was the first to use
A proximity fuse.
The snapdragon's gun
Is a hair-trigger one.

The black bats fly
In a radar sky,
A bee to thistle
Is a guided missile,
And a squid can get
Where it wants by jet.

In the katydid's ode
There's a crude Morse code,

And the submerged loon
Has the schnorkel's boon . . .

Ain't Nature the queer
Old engineer?

Crows in the Corn

The lookout crow
In the big tall pine
Sees the corn I sow,
Sees the corn I grow,
Sees the corn I know
That he sees, and so
Is it his or mine?
Shall he die or dine?
He's a foxy foe;
Every time I hoe
Every hill and row,
Going to and fro
Up and down the line,
There he is, by Joe,
In the big tall pine.
"Cheerio, let's go!"
He will caw, and nine
Black crows say, "O
K? Oh, that's fine."
And they dive in low
On the corn I sow,
On the corn I hoe,
On the corn I grow
For my kith and kine.
And thanks to the crow
In the big tall pine
It has gone like snow,
Like an old bon mot,
Like a tallyho,
Like a glass of wine
In the clear sunshine,
In the long ago.

Cantabrigian

Man from Emmanuel

"Is that you, John Harvard?"
I said to his statue.
"Aye — that's me," said John,
"And after you're gone."

Cambridge Canticles

Cambridge Snow

In Boston when it snows at night
They clean it up by candlelight.
In Cambridge, quite the other way,
It snows and there they leave it lay.

Cambridge Confetti

1

The body undergraduate? Clean
With morning shower. Shift of scene:
The undergraduate body? Sir:
Literate, but a litterer.

2

The cigarette may have its use
When mind must measure things abtruse.
To see the cigarette abstrewn
Is why to dee I'd lay me doon.

3

O cellophane! O paper wrap!
It is with you that I would scrap.
It is from you I raise the eye
To scraps of cloud in Cambridge sky.

Cross Country Footnote

The loveliest of autumn sports
Is running miles in simple shorts;
The coaches never take a chance
On anyone who runs in pants.

Second Half

Shadows are long on Soldiers Field,
Where some of us sit half congealed.
Nature, it seems, the greatest Healer,
Is even greater as Congealer.

Crew Cut

Now as the river fills with ice
The shells are locked up with the mice.
A world of shouts and grunts and groans
Has vanished with the megaphones.

Notes on a Track Meet

Starter

If anyone has fun,
Why that's the starter with his gun —
The which he'd gladly aim
At the jumper of the same.

Century

The lad who runs the 100 yds.,
Accompanied by competing pds.,
Considers it a mighty ft.
If he is hot in every ht. —
But that is rarely on the cds.

Discus

Discus is Greek:
Eke the hibiscus.
You take the thrower:
I'll take the grower.

15′1″

Who climbs the air on slender pole
Assumes a sudden stellar role;
But still he has to cross the bar,
Like Tennyson, to stay a star.

Hurdler

The hurdler minds but doesn't mend his fences,
Which fold the way the Arabs fold their tentses.

4:08 2/5

He wears the best of spikéd shoes,
And runs to win and not to lose,
And times his quarters on the dial
That measures two feet to the mile.

High Jump

Fellow, barefoot, five feet one,
Essays to jump, say, six feet three.
I don't know just how that can be,
But then I've never seen it done.

Hammer

The hammer? Yes, an easy thing
To lift or raise, if not to swing.
But youth must have its fling or flung,
And he who has the hammer swung
Is like to make the welkin ring.

Javelin

The ravell'd sleave of I Don't Care unravellin'
Expresses all my interest in the javelin.

Three Limericks for the Alumni

A young Junior College out west,
Having thirty-five grand to invest,
        Bought 500 shrs.
        Of Dehydrated Prs.
And a filly named Mother-Knows-Best.

At a Class Agent Dinner in North
Philadelphia, the Chairman held forth
        Till a quarter of ten
        On the theme that in Penn.
Every man should give more than he's Swarth.

A native Executive Sec
Of a Fund at Nahuatl Toltec
        Has denied that his needs
        Are for Mexican beads.
Huatl please him? Nahuatl? A chec!

Wings and Things

Mole

Man has an oversoul,
But not the mole.
What the mole has isn't clear,
But it's an undersoul, I fear.

Holstein

I bought a little Holstein calf:
It wasn't Holstein but by half.
And half a Holstein, bull or cow,
I'd call a Halfstein anyhow.

Bunny

The motto of the rabbit?
Amo, amas, amabbit.

Slug

My hand turns over the stone
And there lies the slug alone,
Pale as the darkness made him.
I shall not grade or degrade him.

Lemming

Before condemning
The lemming
One should get on to
Where he's gone to.

Killer

Bloodthirsty,
becurst, he
who durst, he
survives.
So the measly
weasel, he
easily
thrives.

Mantis

The praying mantis doesn't pray:
He simply likes to pose that way.
The sect which he's an insect in
Leads with its left and not the chin.

Leopard Frog

A bog
Is where you find the leopard frog:
The boggier, polliwoggier,
And wetter, the better.
On a log he is bumpy
And jumpy:
Not so
Down below.
Delicately peppered
Like a leopard,
He has lots and lots
Of spots.
He can change one and does:
The one where he was.

Midge

No *te deum*
For this *noceum* —
Latin, you know:
See Thoreau.
What a blighter!
What a biter!

Woodpecker

I hear his little drum upon
The tree that he has come upon.
The tree is dead — this limb of it;
At any rate, the rim of it.
A limb so nicely rabbited
Is sure to be inhabited,
Wherefore the rising decibel
To everyone addressable —
To all now wholly holeable
For whom the bell is tollable.

Utterance on the Otter

Don't he putter or potter?
No. Always on the go.
What about?
Trout.
Vim?
A slide and a swim
Keep him in trim.
Then what?
Not a lot.
He'll spend
Days on end
Playing with a lotter
Other otter.

Skunk

Man is not partial to the skunk
And in his presence has no spunk.
At night within a Buick's beam
Skunks die, yet people do not seem
Delighted when their dry-cell torch
Defines one underneath the porch.
But still of all our fauna he,
The skunk, shows sempiternal glee.
You catch him, when the moon is round,
At play upon the silver ground —
The merriest of little grigs,
And merry even when he digs
For grubs. Why one of such good heart
Is in bad odor from the start
Is more than I'm prepared to say.
Perhaps we'd love him in a way
If his performance glad and gay
Were given as a matinee.

Cod

The cod
Is odd.
The Cape Codder
Is odder.

Gnatty

On the wing
Gnats sing
Gnotes that match
G natch.
When I feel they're sharp,
I gnock 'em flat.
You can tune a harp,
But gnot a gnat.

Walking Stick

This slender bug looks like a twig,
And that to some is *infra dig.*
He's infra something, sure as fate:
A meal? disaster? stick-up? date?

Who Does What

The nuthatch is inclined to nip,
The hummingbird's inclined to sip,
The swallow is inclined to dip,
The osprey is inclined to grip,
The catbird is inclined to quip,
One sparrow is inclined to chip,
The hawk and owl incline to rip,
The snipe is much inclined to snip,
The penguin is inclined to flip,
The whippoorwill inclined to whip,
The shrike I am inclined to skip.

Pelican

The pelican, a totipalmate bird,
Bill very large, distensible gular pouch,
Is really in himself enough absurd.
For anything beyond that, I'll not vouch.

Water Strider

(Family Gerridae)

The water strider deserves mention
For his uplifting invention —
Something to do with surface tension.
Man aestivates
While Gerri skates.
Mistake a lake for a lawn,
And man is gone:
Let the water freeze,
And he's.

May Fly

Unlike the Gerridae
The Ephemeridae
Greatly prefer mating
To skating.

I Says

A saw-whet owl is what I see.
I don't know whet saw he in me.

Bachelor

In the small scale
I admire the snail:
There is no spouse
In his house.

Cacomistle

The Cacomistle or Cacomixle: "A carnivore related to and resembling the racoon."

— Webster

Cacomistle? Cacomixle?
What? *Identical?* Such tricks'll
Make a cacomixle mistle-
Lead you. If it doesn't, this'll.

Sing Cocoon

The little caterpillar creeps
Awhile before in silk it sleeps.
It sleeps awhile before it flies,
And flies awhile before it dies,
And that's the end of three good tries.

Pterosaur

The pterosaur, so leathery of wing,
Was not the feathery kind of bird to sing.
Small wonder it is whither and not whether
He flew into oblivion hell for leather.

On the Oyster

We praise the oyster, cloisterous and true,
Whose normal life's unboisterous and blue.
He chooses not to royster,
And his choiceter be an oyster
Gives him poise the while we foist him on a stew —
Him or missus, much the moister of the two.

Oh, he's smelly, full of jelly, coarse of grain;
But a shelly nonpareilly in the main.
As a worm to vermicelli,
As a Celtic to a Kelly,
He's an oyster from his belly to his brain.
And with six a quorum, may we meet again!

Bowerbird

The bowerbird, Aussie and oscine both,
Builds for himself a "playhouse" — quoth, unquoth —
Or bower used for courting girl bb's.
If any bird's original, then he's.

Jerboa

Jaculus jaculus of northern Africa.

— Webster

Jaculus jaculus,
Nothing miraculous:
Rat of a sort,
Front legs too short,
Hind legs too long;
All rather wrong.
Small kangaroo,
But not for the zoo.
Hard now to class him:
Mind if we pass him?

Field Note

The Imported Cabbage Butterfly
(White with six brown spots)
Dallies over the unimported cabbages
Out and across lots
Like a traveler braving Kansas
With the license plates of Maine,
The sea-sound in the restless corn,
Green-needle music inward borne,
And potatoes on the brain.

Kudu

Who makes a to-do
About the kudu?
I don't.
You do?

Wood Duck

The wood duck builds her sheltered nest
Within a hollow tree above
The water she is thinking of
When summer, like the egg, is mute.
But after all, the water's best:
Her day-old ducklings jump the nest
As sure as peace forsakes the dove.
And maybe it is mother love,
Or maybe they are not distressed,
Or maybe she is just astute
Since maybe it requires a shove
To teach the young idea to chute.

Water Ouzel

Misunderstood and largely mispronounced,
The water ouzel, youzel be advised,
Dives into mountain streams, fresh air renounced,
And *walks* along the bottom. You surprised?

Natter Jack

The natter jack, or running toad,
Is not a subject for an ode.
A toad that runs, a jack that's natter,
Is hardly lyric for that matter.

Vultur Gryphus

Let us ponder
The condor:
Biggest thing
On the wing —
A subject not cultural
But vultural.
Any on view
In the U.S.?
                    A few.
Down in the Andes —
Or up?
            Yep. Some dandies,
But *high.* Where there's *Donder*
Und Blitzen, there's condor:
Bald head and bare neck.
There he is!
                    What! That speck?

Worm

There really isn't very much
To say about the worm as such.
Perhaps a piece on pachyderms
Is better than a word on worms.

Ornithorhynchus

Shoo to a fly,
Scat to a cattypuss.
What is the cry
For a duckbill platypus?

Shoebill

The shoebill hasn't got a shoe,
Nor will he get this billet-doux.

Podilymbus Podiceps

The flicker *does* go *flicker,*
The phoebe *does* say *phoebe.*
A grebe, then *should* say *greeby,*
And I'd know just what he be —
Much quicker.

Shape

The mouth of a fledgling
Is a wedgling.

Grub

I do not recommend the grub —
The young of *what?* Aye, there's the rub!
The fox and bear, they have a cub;
Wings on the loose produce a grub.

Giraffe

Two staffs make staves.
Two giraffes don't make giraves.
One giraffe
Makes one laugh.

Foolish Guillemot

Is it: "There goes a guillemo?"
Or "Who's got a guillemot?"
Do *I* know, do *I* know?
What?
        I do not.

Point of View

The little bat hangs upside down,
And downside up the possum.
To show a smile they have to frown,
Say those who've run across 'em.

Contentment

The cat purrs,
The murre murrs;
The bee, when comfy,
Is humfy.

Salamander

The salamander lives as far
From fire as I live from a star.
In fact, you'll find he lives alone
And out of sight beneath a stone
Beside a brook, a lake, or pond.
Of salamanders who is fond?

Who's Ooze

There's always the clam:
He's not what I am,
I'm not what he is.
Gee whiz —
Not mentally!
But incidentally,
Damme,
I come from the clammy
Cold sea
Same as he.
My chassis is classic,
His is Jurassic.
I did what he does,
He is what I was.
I got ahead,
He stayed in bed.
I made the break,
He the mistake.
So I don't give a damn
For the clam!
I'm choosy:
He's oozy.

Sloth

So loath to praise the sloth am I,
I do not think that I shall try.
In fact, this silly edentate
Deserves the uncongenial fate
Of sleeping through his nights and days
Without the benefit of praise.

Ω

The inchworm
Doesn't squirm,
Nor is that comic actor
A caterpillar tractor.
He gives himself a hunch
To move his prolegs in a bunch.
Whatever the route,
His epilegs follow suit;
And while he plays his hunches
He lunches.

Matriculation

Anadromous, the common shad
Swims up the river just to add,
According to his golden rule,
A freshman class to that old school
Of which he is himself a grad.

Shore Patrol

Catadromous, they say of eels,
That leave fresh water for the salt.
Sinbadromous, the sailor reels
Away from water to the malt.

Dodo

The dodo that died-o
Is *Didus ineptus.*
In modo he tried-o
But couldn't accept us.

Funny Businence

The Trickless Trolley

She took the trickless trolley
To meet with supperman;
The road was stoop and holly,
She swipt through dole and glan.

But supperman was biding
By trickless trolley stap.
This was the leaf! Exziding!
No transfear — end of trap!

Brave supperman, thy garlie
Did sieve thee dime or two.
Fess up to err thus squarly
When wid to wan so true.

Foray at 4 A.M.

I tangled with a tangy cheese,
And zestful as beyond my need,
I sought the cereals. Of these,
Exploded oleander seed:

Smooth, crunchable, and under lip
As tasty as red sidr bark,
Enlarged my courage and my grip
On life. And then, to fan the spark,

I covered carbonitrous bread
With pixcephalic jellied squid.
From there the conflagration spread.
Don't chide me now, for I've been chid.

Roc

The eg of the roc
Is out of stoc.
If not, I beg
Your pardon, eg.

O lad, O las,
Things come, things pas:
The shattered shel,
The roc himsel.

Funny Businence

O Assonance!
Music of dissonance,
Angler of incinence,
Jongleur of juicynance,
Yessir of resonance,
Nosir of reasonance,
Ichor of listenance,
Liquor of licenance,
Checker of chessonance,
Carbonate bisonance:
Skoal to your skill!
Scale to your skirl!
Squirrel to your school!
(O drooly good drool!)

Pal as in peal
Lisle as in loll
Wail as in wool
Hep as in hip
Neap as in nape
Nap as in nope
(Damn dippy good dope!)

O Assonance,
Incross in puissonance!
Fire gives me fore,
Far gave me fur,
Fare guv me fear.
(I feel queer,
I feel quare.)

Assonance, assonance!
Blessonance, blessonance!

Psychoinsomnia

Matter of fact, he never went back home,
But wrote a note and played his palindrome
And lit the candles on the capstan bars
And had a nightmare calling stalling cars.
Queer, that was it. But not so vast my friend:
He came a sudden of a sodden end.
Before he had the time to crease the cash,
His battery was deader than the flash;
And only in such vestiges of trace
Do we remember how he had a face.
There was no notice. In his naïve town
A flag was flown. At dusk they shook it down.

As to All That

I should like to say again
What I haven't said before:
First the egg and then the hen
And then the egg and what's the score?
Little more,
Little more.

There's a star beyond the void,
There's the void beyond a star,
And a child is much annoyed
If you pursue the thing that far.
Au revoir,
Au revoir!

A Hex on the Mexican X

Returned from Mehiko he'll grab,
If he has luck, a tahikab.
And shouting to the driver: "Son,"
He'll shout, "make haste to Lehington

And Sihy-first." And now he's there,
Ehaling fresh monohide air.
Manhattan leaps from plinth of stone;
His soul sings like a sahophone.

Shenanigans

1

O xenolithic Eliot,
Bejabberwocky Joyce,
Ineffable affiliate,
Vasdeferential voice:
  Animula
  Vagula
  Glandula
I plays on me bhroken mandula
Hosanna Livia Plurabellee,
Hello to the hollowing men from me!

2

Something too much — he said it was too much;
The orator who said it was too small.
And touchy too. The touchiness of touch
Is something some can't hardly bide at all.
A tall dark fellow disagreed with that:
With that we gave it up. Upparently
They thought it was the smilax on the cat,
But cats don't smile, alax, as you can see.
Come Thistlemas the grass may trim too thick.
But there it is. Wave bye now! It's no trick.

3

Finnegans Wake
Is the tarpit lake
Where the scibertoth words went down.
In the dream I drum
By the skimmery scum

Of the old Dipdobbelin town:
There was Syllabub Sib
And little Ad Lib
And old Dan Tucker with his plastic bib
And the crone with the crinoline crown.

4

As I was perning in the gyre,
I met a man from Invershire.
"I do not yearn to pern," said he.
But inasmuch as Innisfree,
"I wish to pern," said I at once.
And so the cap will fit the dunce,
And so the golden apples burn
The while I'll tell you how to pern.

Fancier Mr. Fenn

The paltry poultry of that Mr. Fenn
Consisted of three Dorkings, one lame duck,
Two bantam roosters, an instructive hen
Reduced in old age to a klaxon cluck.

His geese were five — a gaggle, if you will;
A flock of Orpingtons with feathered legs.
He favored most his gamecocks Jeff and Bill
Unless he found them sitting on glass eggs.

An odd assortment: single and rose comb,
One webfoot cycling round that precious pond;
And Mr. Fenn, a flightless little gnome,
Always a quack behind, a crow beyond.

Remembrance of Things Passed

Then the monumental suppers
In the menumontal style,
With the closing of the uppers
On the pattridge and the quile;

And the little twinge of ispic
On the laminated leaf
Of the lettuces — the crispic
Kind to chlorophyll the beef.

Such a cetalogue of coctions,
Such comastible display!
Such bemumbled introdoctions,
Such a tryranny of tray!

At the chafing dish the chafir,
Round the rustic mousse the moose;
Mrs. Pringle nips a wafer
Etched in *pâté* from the goose.

Now the corks in jet propulsion,
In some syllables a toast;
All exult in last exulsion:
Eggsit X, eggshausted host!